ROME

2021
Restaurants

The Food Enthusiast's
Long Weekend Guide

Andrew Delaplaine

Andrew Delaplaine is the Food Enthusiast.
When he's not playing tennis,
he dines anonymously
at the Publisher's (considerable) expense.

GET 3 FREE NOVELS
Like political thrillers?
See next page to download 3 great page-turners—
FREE - no strings attached.

Copyright © by Gramercy Park Press - All rights reserved.

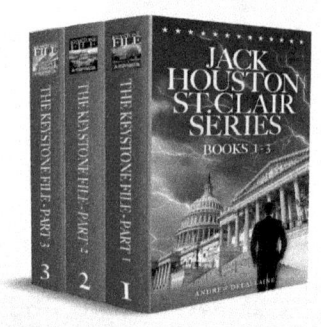

WANT 3 FREE THRILLERS?
Why, of course you do!
If you like these writers--
Vince Flynn, Brad Thor, Tom Clancy, James Patterson, David Baldacci, John Grisham, Brad Meltzer, Daniel Silva, Don DeLillo
If you like these TV series –
House of Cards, Scandal, West Wing, The Good Wife, Madam Secretary, Designated Survivor

You'll love the **unputdownable** series about Jack Houston St. Clair, with political intrigue, romance, and loads of action and suspense.

Besides writing travel books, I've written political thrillers for many years that have delighted hundreds of thousands of readers. I want to introduce you to my work!
Send me an email and I'll send you a link where you can download the first 3 books in my bestselling series, absolutely FREE.

Mention **this book** when you email me.
andrewdelaplaine@mac.com

Copyright © Gramercy Park Press.
Please submit corrections, additions or comments to gppress@gmail.com

Table of Contents

Introduction – 5

Chapter 1
The A to Z Listings – 13
Ridiculously Extravagant
Sensible Alternatives
Quality Bargain Spots

Chapter 2
Nightlife – 66

Chapter 3
Shopping – 68

Index – 73

Other Books
by the Food Enthusiast – 80

INTRODUCTION

DID YOU FIND AN INTERESTING PLACE?
If you discover a place you think I should check out on my next visit, drop me a line, will you? I'll mention your name if I end up listing it.
andrewdelaplaine@mac.com

"When in Rome do as the Romans do," and that means enjoying the wonderful food. Visiting Rome may be as much about the food as it is about visiting the museums and historical landmarks. A trip to Rome is certainly not complete without experiencing the food and drink at the many colorful trattorias,

pizzerias, ristorantes and gelaterias. For many years Rome's restaurant scene remained the same and you could stop by a favorite eatery for mounds of pasta but there's been a recent explosion of new restaurants, Panini shops, street-food stalls, bakeries, and cocktail bars run by a new generation of Romans who are adding a new flavor to the ancient city.

Traveling the winding streets of Rome you will find many Italian restaurants in tourist centers. While most restaurants in Rome offer the native cuisine you will also find eateries offering Chinese, Mexican, Indian, and Thai food but beware, the standard is not as high as you will find in other major cities. Once you try the cuisine at the traditional Italian restaurants you probably won't care to try anything else, anyway.

The best way to see Rome is to walk, since the transportation can be a bit unreliable, and you can discover so much more on foot. You'll see a whole world that could never be described in any tour book. You'll be lured by the salespeople, the aroma of a bakery, and possibly find a hidden piazza that seems right out of the 16th century (because it is). You'll wander through neighborhoods filled with families and shops.

There are restaurants everywhere but you should know a few things before heading out for a meal. First, realize that the Italians have a timetable with restaurants opening for lunch from noon to around 3 p.m., and dinner doesn't begin until 7 p.m. Since the Italians usually don't eat until 9 p.m., it's advisable to dine eat early to avoid the crowds and most likely you'll also be dining with other tourists. (If you want to eat with the locals, the later you eat, the better.)

Most of the restaurants located on the main squares may offer great views but the better and less expensive eateries are usually located on small streets away from the bustling crowds. For the most part, avoid restaurants that have waiters aggressively trying to lure customers into their venue or passing out flyers. The good restaurants don't need hawkers.

Once inside, don't expect the waitstaff to be as friendly as waiters in America. Waiters are there to do a job and will recite the specials, explain certain dishes, and will even help you select a wine for your meal. Italian menus are divided into courses. Italians often order one course at a time. They approach food in a much more relaxed and (some, including myself, would use the word "civilized") manner. They eat it and then order another course if they're still hungry. Don't look for a lot of those Italian dishes that you're use to seeing at your local Italian eatery at home because many are not authentic Italian so they won't be on any menu here in Rome. Personally, I always make a habit to asking for any specials if they are not offered because often they are some of the freshest and best dishes you can get. If there are specials, I always select one over anything on the menu. Always.

Getting the bill and tipping. Italians take their time eating and dining is never rushed. You may have to ask for the check as they consider it rude to drop down a check immediately after a meal is finished. Don't be surprised if it takes a good 15 minutes for the check to arrive after it has been requested. Note that in Rome, the waiters are paid a good wage and do not count on tips. Romans generally leave a euro per two people for a meal but many restaurants add a service charge so then you don't leave a tip. Tips should be left in cash because they don't offer an option to add a tip to a credit card charge.

Enjoy the sites of Rome, see the Coliseum, the Roman Forum, enjoy Sunday morning shopping at the Porta Portese flea market, toss a coin in the Trevi

Fountain, and climb to the top of St. Peter's Basilica. Those things will all help work up an appetite but nothing gets your stomach churning more than the aromas in the air from the bakeries, the pizzerias, and the outdoor cafes. Eating authentic Italian cuisine is an experience and nothing like eating at your neighborhood Italian restaurant.

When in Rome, there are dishes that you can't leave without trying. Authentic Carbonara is the best and **Al Moro**, a restaurant located near the Trevi Fountain, is famous for its Carbonara. Italians rave about the deep fried crispy artichokes, so venture into the Jewish quarter and try this delicacy. The Italians are known for their pizza and they offer several varieties. Pizza Bianca, different than American pizza, is made with focaccia style pizza bread served in local bakeries. The Roman style thin crust pizza, not the pizza from Naples served mostly in the U.S., features a thin crust that's cooked crispy without the crust lip around the edges. While many American cities now feature gelato shops, they are nothing like authentic tartufo or gelato. Real Italian gelato is never fluffed up or disguised with artificial colors or chemicals. Tartufo, a popular dessert made famous by **Tre Scalini** in Piazza Navona, is a dessert made of one or two flavors with frozen fruit in the center and covered with a shell of chocolate.

It's true that Rome is overflowing with restaurants but like anywhere else in the world, many are overpriced, mediocre, and cater to unsuspecting tourists. Beware of the eateries that are filled with tourists only. Even in Rome you can order bad pizza and generic gelato.

The
A to Z Listings
Ridiculously Extravagant
Sensible Alternatives
Quality Bargain Spots

DID YOU FIND AN INTERESTING PLACE?
If you discover a place you think I should check out on my next visit, drop me a line, will you? I'll mention your name if I end up listing it.
andrewdelaplaine@mac.com

ALFREDO ALLA SCROFA
Via della Scrofa 104A, Rome, +39 06 68806163
www.alfredoallascrofa.com
CUISINE: Italian/Mediterranean/Seafood
DRINKS: Full Bar
SERVING: Lunch & Dinner

PRICE RANGE: $$$
NEIGHBORHOOD: Centro Storico
This 1907 romantic eatery is known as the birthplace of fettuccini Alfredo. Favorites: Fettuccine Alfredo and Beef Carpaccio. Nice variety of wines.

ANTICO FORNO AI SERPENTI
Via dei Serpenti, 122-123, Rome, +39 06 4542 7920
www.anticofornoaiserpenti.it
CUISINE: Bakery
DRINKS: No Booze
SERVING: Breakfast & Lunch
PRICE RANGE: $$
NEIGHBORHOOD: Monti
With the atmosphere of a French bistro, this eatery offers baked goods and pizza. The treats include pies, cakes, panettone, puffs, and delicious espresso. If it's in season, get the pumpkin and gorgonzola panino. Popular among tourists, but not a tourist trap at all.

ARMANDO AL PANTHEON
Salita dè Crescenzi, 31, +39 06 6880 3034
www.armandoalpantheon.it
CUISINE: Roman
DRINKS: Full Bar
SERVING: Lunch, Dinner; closed Sun
PRICE RANGE: $$$
NEIGHBORHOOD: Centro Storico
This popular family run eatery offers a menu of classic and creative Roman cuisine. Some of the best traditional cooking you're going to find in Rome. Though it's right in what I would call "Tourist Trap Alley," don't let that fool you. Locals still come here in droves because the food's so good and they like the wood-paneled interior and wine list with fair prices. Vegetarian dishes are available. Menu favorites include Black rice with seafood, amatriciana, carbonara and Lasagna. Oh, let's not forget the *torta*

antic aroma, a dish filled with fruit that's rather like strawberry shortcake, only better.

AROMA
PALAZZO MANFREDI HOTEL
Via Labicana, 125, Rome, +39 06 97615109
www.aromarestaurant.it
CUISINE: Modern Cuisine
DRINKS: Full Bar
SERVING: Lunch, Dinner
PRICE RANGE: $$$$
NEIGHBORHOOD: Esquilino
Located at Palazzo Manfredi Hotel, diners are treated to amazing views of Ancient Rome while enjoying the incredible cuisine of a 5-Diamond restaurant. Menu favorites include: Sea Bass and salmon duo with crispy king prawns and Chianina beef fillet in red wine. Impressive wine selection. An unforgettable dining experience.

AROMATICUS
Via Urbana, 134, 00184 Roma, +39 06 488 1355
www.aromaticus.it/
CUISINE: Juice Bar/Salads
DRINKS: Beer & Wine Only
SERVING: Lunch, Dinner; closed Mon
PRICE RANGE: $$$
NEIGHBORHOOD: Monti
This urban farming and aromatic herb shop sells aromatic plants, edible flowers, sprouts, salts, exotic peppers in the front of the house, while in the room at the rear you'll find a little kitchen serving a menu of salads, steak or fish tartare and Carpaccio. Select wine selection.

BAFFETTO
Via del Governo Vecchio, 114, 00186 Roma, Italy
+39 06 686 1617
www.pizzeriabaffetto.it
CUISINE: Pizza

DRINKS: Beer & Wine Only
SERVING: Lunch Wed, Sat & Sun, Dinner nightly, closed Tuesday
PRICE RANGE: $$
NEIGHBORHOOD: Centro Storico
This little pizzeria features Roman-style, thin & crispy pizzas. Favorites include: Pizza marguerite and Pizza Baffetta. No Reservations. No cash.

BAR DEL FICO
Piazza del Fico 26, Rome, +39 06 68891373
www.bardelfico.com/en/
CUISINE: Café/Italian
DRINKS: Full Bar

SERVING: Breakfast, Lunch, & Dinner
PRICE RANGE: $$
NEIGHBORHOOD: Centro Storico/Parione
This funky eatery is one of Rome's hottest restaurants. The place has a charming bar area and is a popular late-night hangout. Affordable charcuterie platters, smart cocktails. Reservations recommended.

BIR & FUD
Via Benedetta 23, Rome, +39 06 5894016
www.birandfud.it
CUISINE: Pizza
DRINKS: Beer & Wine Only
SERVING: Lunch, Dinner
PRICE RANGE: $$
NEIGHBORHOOD: Trastevere
This trendy pizzeria offers great pizza and homemade potato chips. The bar offers a large selection of tap beers including American craft beers, German, Belgian, and other European beers.

CACIO E PEPE
Via Giuseppe Avezzana 11, Rome, +39 06 3217268
www.trattoriacacioepepeprati.com
CUISINE: Italian
DRINKS: Beer & Wine Only
SERVING: Lunch & Dinner; Lunch only on Saturdays; closed Sundays
PRICE RANGE: $$
NEIGHBORHOOD: Prati
Intimate rustic (OK, it's definitely down market and kind of beat-up, but I love it) trattoria serving classic Italian fare. They have a handwritten menu, but opt for the signature dish that gives this place its name— *cacio e pepe* (basically, just cheese & black pepper, but unlike you've ever had it before unless you've been here). Other favorites: Bruchetta with ricotta cheese and Eggplant lasagna. Street dining on the heated sidewalk terrace for the ultimate Rome experience.

CAFÉ DONEY
Via Vittorio Veneto 141, Rome, +39 06 47082783
www.restaurantdoney.com
CUISINE: Italian
DRINKS: Beer & Wine Only
SERVING: Breakfast, Lunch & Dinner
PRICE RANGE: $$$
NEIGHBORHOOD: Termini
Casual but luxurious eatery offering creative menu of Italian fare. Favorites: Roasted loin of rabbit and Pasta with squid and cherry tomatoes. Nice wine selection.

CASINE VALADIER
Piazza Bucarest, Rome, +39 06 6992 2090
www.casinavaladier.com
CUISINE: Italian
DRINKS: Full Bar
SERVING: Lunch & Dinner; closed Mon
PRICE RANGE: $$$$
Upscale Italian eatery featuring breathtaking views of Rome from the terrace. Some have argued that this is the best view in Rome, and I am not one to argue. It's in a majestic villa next to the Borghese Gardens. The view extends from the capacious balcony as well as the ground-floor terrace from where you can get spectacular views. Try to come here on a Sunday where the brunch is long, leisurely and relaxing. (Plan on two hours.) Though it's not always on the menu, the chef's special dish (a fillet of beef with foie gras) can always be ordered. Great desserts and wine selection.

CHECCHINO DAL 1887
Via di Monte Testaccio 30, Rome, +39 06 5743816
www.checchino-dal-1887.com
CUISINE: Roman
DRINKS: Beer & Wine Only
SERVING: Dinner; closed Mondays
PRICE RANGE: $$$
NEIGHBORHOOD: Ostiense, Testaccio
Beautiful refined eatery offering an upscale dining experience. The friend who brought me here wanted me to try the tripe with a soupy tomato mix, but I draw the line at tripe. Can't stand the stuff. However,

I fell in love with the Bruschetta with pecorino & sage and Oxtail. Impressive wine selection (quite a few local wines, also) and rich desserts. Try the Panna cotta – a cream custard with berry sauce.

COROMANDEL
Via di Monte Giordano 60, Rome, +39 06 68802461
www.coromandel.it
CUISINE: Brasseries
DRINKS: Full Bar
SERVING: Breakfast, Lunch, & Dinner; closed Mon
PRICE RANGE: $$$
NEIGHBORHOOD: Centro Storico
This cute little restaurant (with pale pink walls) offers a lovely décor and delicious food. This is one of the best spots for breakfast in the area. Nice selection of pizzas and you can order by the slice. The dinner

menu is prix fixe, with excellent seasonal dishes like red snapper. The atmosphere is very relaxed, you can even read a book here without a complaint from the staff.

CRISTALLI DI ZUCCHERO
Via di Val Tellina 114, Rome, +39 06 58230323
https://www.ristorantevelavevodetto.it/prenota-quiriti-online.html
CUISINE: Bakery
DRINKS: Full Bar
SERVING: Breakfast/Brunch
PRICE RANGE: $$
NEIGHBORHOOD: Portuense
If you're in search of delicious sweets then you've found the place. The offerings include a variety of macaroons, cakes, cannolis, and a menu of tasty appetizers.

DA CESARE
Via del Casaletto 45, Rome, +39 06 536015
www.trattoriadacesare.it/?lang=en

CUISINE: Roman
DRINKS: Beer & Wine Only
SERVING: Lunch & Dinner; closed Wednesdays
PRICE RANGE: $$$
NEIGHBORHOOD: Portuense
Small neighborhood restaurant perched high upon a hill, where people come for the food, definitely not the décor. While the restaurant itself isn't much to look at (and who cares anyway, right?), the views you get up here are worth the trip. Favorites: Pasta alla Gricia (best pasta in the world) and Eggplant Croquettes (a great starter, like nothing you've ever had before). I never leave without sampling their superior fritto misto. Reservations recommended.

DA ENZO AL 29
Via dei Vascellari 29, Rome, +39 06 5812260
www.daenzoal29.com
CUISINE: Roman
DRINKS: Beer & Wine Only
SERVING: Lunch & Dinner; closed Sundays
PRICE RANGE: $$
NEIGHBORHOOD: Trastevere
A simple small eatery serving Roman classics. Outdoor seating offers the best café experience watching the crowds while dining. Favorites: Fettucine with mussels and clams and Coda alla vaccinara (Oxtail). Always a wait, but worth it.

DAL BOLOGNESE
Piazza del Popolo 1, Rome, +39 06 3222799
www.dalbolognese.it
CUISINE: Pizza, Mediterranean

DRINKS: Beer & Wine Only
SERVING: Lunch & Dinner; closed Mondays
PRICE RANGE: $$$$
NEIGHBORHOOD: Flaminio
Elegant restaurant serving high-end, expensive Italian cuisine. Go upstairs to the smoking room where you can also get a drink before dinner. Favorites: Tagliatelle alla Bolognese and the Milanese (served with pure mashed potatoes). Try their Tiramisu – a different version that most serve. Nice wine selection.

DITIRANBO
Piazza della Cancelleria, 74-75, Rome, +39 06 687 1626
www.ristoranteditirambo.it
CUISINE: Italian
DRINKS: Beer & Wine Only
SERVING: Breakfast, Lunch, & Dinner
PRICE RANGE: $$$
NEIGHBORHOOD: Centro Storico
This small trattoria just a bit north of the Campo de' Fiori offers a menu of seasonal and creative Roman classics in a charming atmosphere with wood-beamed ceilings. Here you'll find great antipasti and unexpected treats like Gorgonzola-pear soufflé. (Large vegetarian selection.) Menu favorites include: Roast Lamb and Suckling pig. Impressive wine list of over 500 labels.

EATALY
Piazzale XII Ottobre 1492, Rome, +39 06 90279201
www.roma.eataly.it
CUISINE: Italian
DRINKS: Full Bar
SERVING: Lunch, Dinner
PRICE RANGE: $$$
NEIGHBORHOOD: Ostiense
If you've been to their location in NYC, you know what to expect...a food shrine to Italian cuisine. Here you'll find pasta, wines, cheese, prosciutto, pesce, coffee, espresso, gelato, and more. Eat here or shop to take home. There are 4 or 5 aisles of just dried pasta. This location includes 23 restaurants, bakeries, a gelateria and a rosticceria.

ENOTECA FERRARA
Piazza Trilussa, 41, Rome, +39 06 5833 3920
www.enotecaferrara.it
CUISINE: Italian
DRINKS: Full Bar
SERVING: Lunch, Dinner
PRICE RANGE: $$$$
NEIGHBORHOOD: Trastevere
This upscale eatery offers an impressive menu of Italian fare, pretty rare in this neighborhood these days. Menu favorites include: Grilled Lamb chops and Homemade large chestnut fettuccine. This wine bar, restaurant and gastronomic boutique impress customers with its award-winning wine list.

FELICE
Via Mastro Giorgio, 29, Rome, +39 06 574 6800
www.feliceatestaccio.it
CUISINE: Roman
DRINKS: Beer & Wine Only
SERVING: Lunch, Dinner
PRICE RANGE: $$$
NEIGHBORHOOD: Testaccio, Ostiense
Open since 1936, this celebrated trattoria features a menu of authentic Roman pasta dishes and other favorites. The food doesn't get more "traditional" than it is here. Celebs like Roberto Benigni are regulars, so they've been doing something right all these years. The tables are packed tightly together, so if you're claustrophobic, be warned! Menu highlights include: Cacio e pepe and Amatriciana pasta. Get a twist on the usual Carbonara by ordering the spaghetti with cheese and pepper – they toss it right at your

table. The roasted lamb is superior. Reservations are a must in this always-crowded place.

FIASCHETTERIA BELTRAMME
39 Via della Croce, Rome, +39 06 6979 7200
www.fiaschetteriabeltramme.info **WEBSITE DOWN**
CUISINE: Italian
DRINKS: Full Bar
SERVING: Lunch & Dinner
PRICE RANGE: $$
Family restaurant featuring Italian classics, including delicious homemade pastas, served in a very laid-back homey atmosphere. I like the tonnarelli especially. What sets this place apart is the great art that hangs on the walls. It's a special dining experience.

FLAVIO AI VELAVEVEDOTTO
Via di Monte Testaccio, 97, Rome, +39 06 574 4194

www.flavioalvelavevodetto.it
WEBSITE DOWN AT PRESS TIME
CUISINE: Roman
DRINKS: Beer & Wine Only
SERVING: Lunch, Dinner
PRICE RANGE: $$$
NEIGHBORHOOD: Testaccio, Ostiense
This unusual eatery is actually located in a centuries-old warehouse built into the "mountain of discarded clay pots," the city's most historic landfill. Menu highlights include: Cacio e Pepe, the Amatriciana, and the Carbonara, suckling pig, oxtail. Note: Menu is completely in Italian but the waitresses will make suggestions. Reservations recommended.

GINA
Via di San Sebastianello, 7A, Rome, +39 33 530 4277
https://ristoexpert.com/migliori-ristoranti/roma/gina
CUISINE: Italian
DRINKS: Full Bar
SERVING: Lunch, Dinner; closed
PRICE RANGE: $$$$
NEIGHBORHOOD: Parioli
GINA, a combination of the owner's names, offers a unique Italian eatery that promotes their passion for food. The menu features bruschetta, salads, sandwiches, pastries, gelato, and yogurt. In winter the restaurant offers fully stocked gourmet picnic baskets prepared for those headed to Villa Borghese Park.

GINGER
Via Borgognona, 43-44, Rome, +39 06 6994 0836
www.ginger.roma.it
CUISINE: Breakfast
DRINKS: Full Bar
SERVING: Breakfast & Lunch
PRICE RANGE: $$
NEIGHBORHOOD: Centro Storico
A nice alternative to the traditional trattoria, this Los Angeles-style eatery with its high-top marble tables and white tile décor offers a creative menu off baguette sandwiches, gnocchi, tortellini, smoothies, and homemade desserts. Here you'll also find an impressive variety of fresh fruit and vegetable juices. Menu available in English or Italian.

GLASS HOSTARIA
Vicolo Dè Cinque, Rome, +39 06 5833 5903
https://glasshostaria.it
CUISINE: Italian

DRINKS: Full Bar
SERVING: Dinner; closed Sun & Mon
PRICE RANGE: $$$$
NEIGHBORHOOD: Trastevere
Though it's in a Medieval building, the design of this slick and chic eatery is ultra-modern, and it offers an impressive upscale dining destination. A very with-it kind of crowd. Experimental items are featured, like risotto with saffron, wild fennel, anise and goat cheese; scallops with koji; rack of lamb with burnt onions and cherries. The tiramisu comes with chocolate crumble—like you've never had before.

GREEN T
Via del Piè di Marmo, 28, Rome, +39 06 679 8628
www.green-tea.it
CUISINE: Chinese
DRINKS: Beer & Wine Only
SERVING: Lunch, Dinner; closed Sun
PRICE RANGE: $$$
NEIGHBORHOOD: Centro Storico
This upscale Chinese restaurant offers and beautiful décor and great food. Menu favorites include: Sweet & Sour Pork and Peking Duck.

IL CONVIVIO TROIANI
Vicolo dei Soldati, 31, +39 06 686 9432
http://www.ilconviviotroiani.it/
CUISINE: Italian
DRINKS: Beer & Wine Only
SERVING: Dinner; closed Sunday
PRICE RANGE: $$
NEIGHBORHOOD: Centro Storico
Beautiful eatery with a semi-private entrance (ring the doorbell) and you're welcomed into a lovely room filled with art and frescoes. Imaginative tasting menus. If you order a la carte, get the spaghetti with garlic and olive oil, spiced with chile, lemon, mint, almonds and pecorino. Unlike any spaghetti dish you've ever had, I promise.
Other menu picks: Squab liver in a cherry and Squab consommé. Nice wine pairings.

IL MARGUTTA
Via Margutta, 118, Rome, +39 06 3265 0577
www.ilmargutta.bio
CUISINE: Vegetarian
DRINKS: Beer & Wine Only
SERVING: Lunch, Dinner; open daily
PRICE RANGE: $$$
NEIGHBORHOOD: Flaminio
This unique eatery features a café and bar with a buffet area located between the two. Food varies from Greek, Indian and Italian. Nice vegetarian options. Great spot for brunch or lunch. This place is also an art gallery.

IL PAGLIACCIO
Via dei Banchi Vecchi 129A, Rome, +39 06 68809595
www.ristoranteilpagliaccio.com

CUISINE: Italian
DRINKS: Full Bar
SERVING: Lunch, Dinner
PRICE RANGE: $$$$
NEIGHBORHOOD: Centro Storico

Chef/owner Anthony Genovese offers a menu of true Roman cuisine served in an attractive intimate space. Menu favorites include great pastas and fish dishes. The desserts are quite creative like the brown bread ice cream and caramel chocolate truffle. Impressive wine menu offers more that 500 labels. Advance book of a month prior required.

IL SORPASSO
31 Via Properzia, Rome, +39 06 8902 4554
www.sorpasso.info
CUISINE: Italian
DRINKS: Full Bar
SERVING: Breakfast & Lunch; closed Sundays
PRICE RANGE: $
NEIGHBORHOOD: Prati

A short walk from the Vatican is this favorite where locals hang out after work. Filled with neighborhood regulars who come for the cheap wine and cheap Italian favorites. Go by for lunch and get a charcuterie board featuring some of the in-house cured meats and wide selection of cheeses.

IL TEMPIO DI ISIDE
11 Via Pietro Verri, Rome, +39 06 700 4741
www.isideristorante.it
CUISINE: Mediterranean
DRINKS: Full Bar
SERVING: Lunch & Dinner
PRICE RANGE: $$$$

Only a few minutes' walk from the Colosseum. It may be listed in some publications as a tourist spot, this is also a locals' favorite. The owners go every morning to the local "fish auction" to get the freshest catch. Menu picks include: Fried baby octopus' tentacles and Langoustine and Prawn. Nice selection of wine. Reservations recommended.

IL VERO ALFREDO
Piazza Augusto Imperatore 30, Rome, +39 06 6878734
www.ilveroalfredo.it
CUISINE: Italian
DRINKS: Full Bar
SERVING: Lunch & Dinner, Dinner only on Mondays
PRICE RANGE: $$$
NEIGHBORHOOD: Centro Storico

Known as the birthplace of Fettuccine Alfredo (though there are other places that claim credit), their version is made with housemade pasta and is creamy and well flavored. People travel the world to sample the Fettuccine Alfredo here. Also impressive is the famous "gold cutlery" donated in 1927 by actors Mary Pickford and Douglas Fairbanks. I send people here to get the experience, but I don't go here myself anymore. Very expensive.

IVO
Via di San Francesco a Ripa 158, Rome, +39 06 5817082
https://ivoatrastevere.it
CUISINE: Italian/Pizza
DRINKS: Full Bar
SERVING: Dinner, Lunch also on Saturday closed Tuesdays
PRICE RANGE: $$
NEIGHBORHOOD: Trastevere

Simple pizzeria serving Roman-style pizzas. Very unassuming but you're here for the pizzas. Nice pasta dishes as well, but skip them for the pizza. Fair to good wine selection.

L'ARCANGELO
Via Giuseppe Gioachino Belli, +39 06 3210992
www.larcangelo.com/
CUISINE: Italian
DRINKS: Full bar
SERVING: Lunch/Dinner/Late Night; closed Sunday
PRICE RANGE: $$$
NEIGHBORHOOD: Prati
Nice upscale eatery with a menu that includes English translations of each dish. Great Italian fare and they are known for serving the best Gnocchi (with Amatriciana sauce) in Rome. (Well, one of the top 10, anyway.) There's also this very flavorful salad: Viaggio a Rocca Priora, which refers to a trip to the chef's hometown—it's got mixed greens wth poached egg spiced with fennel, cumin, licorice. For dessert, I heartily recommend the Beignets Stuffed with Citrus Custard and Caramel. Reservations recommended.

LA BUVETTE
44 Via Vittoria, Rome, +39 06 679 0383
No Website
CUISINE: Italian/Breakfast
DRINKS: No Booze
SERVING: Breakfast, Lunch & Dinner
PRICE RANGE: $$$
On a quiet side street is this endearing café, a traditional old world eatery featuring classic local Italian dishes with sidewalk seating you'll want to take advantage of in good weather. Nice wine pairings.

LA CAMPANA
Vicolo della Campana 18, Rome, +39 06 6875273
www.ristorantelacampana.com
CUISINE: Roman
DRINKS: Full Bar

SERVING: Dinner; closed Mondays
PRICE RANGE: $$
NEIGHBORHOOD: Centro Storico
Known as the oldest restaurant in Rome (dating to 1518), so dining here is definitely an experience not to be rushed. Family-friendly food (and prices). Favorites: Roasted chicken and Pasta ai carciofi (pasta with artichokes).

LA MONTECARLO
Vicolo Savelli, 13, Rome, +39 06 686 1877
www.lamontecarlo.it
CUISINE: Pizza
DRINKS: Full Bar
SERVING: Lunch, Dinner; closed Sun
PRICE RANGE: $$
NEIGHBORHOOD: Trastevere
Popular with locals, this pizzeria offers an impressive variety of thin-crust pizza, pastas, bruschetta, and canapés. Favorites include the Parma Prosciutto Pizza and Wild Mushroom Fettuccini. Desserts are homemade.

LA PERGOLA
Via Alberto Cadlolo, 101, Rome, +39 06 3509 2152
www.romecavalieri.it
CUISINE: Italian
DRINKS: Full Bar
SERVING: Lunch, Dinner; closed Mon
PRICE RANGE: $$$$
NEIGHBORHOOD: Balduina/Montemario
Known as one of the best restaurants in Rome boasting a three-Michelin star rating, this popular eatery also features a wine cellar with over 60,000 bottles. Menu favorites include: Ravioli stuffed with carbonara sauce and Cod with broccoli and salt cod snow. The stunning view alone is worth the visit.

LA FOCACCIA
Via della Pace, 11, Rome, +39 06 9761 7557
www.1stmuse.com/focaccia

CUISINE: Italian/Pizza
DRINKS: Full Bar
SERVING: Lunch, Dinner
PRICE RANGE: $$
NEIGHBORHOOD: Centro Storico
Decorated with exposed brickwork and beamed ceilings, this casual eatery offers more than the great wood-fired pizzas. Here you'll also find delicious pasta and roasted meat dishes, all under the looming edifice of Bramante's gorgeous Santa Maria della Pace church. Whenever visitors drag me into the church so they can have a well-deserved look, I bring them here afterwards. They all love it.

LA TAVERNE DEI FORI IMPERIALI
Via della Madonna dei Monti, 9, Rome, +39 06 679 8643
www.latavernadeiforiimperiali.com
CUISINE: Italian
DRINKS: Beer & Wine Only
SERVING: Lunch, Dinner
PRICE RANGE: $$
NEIGHBORHOOD: Monti, Centro Storico
Located in the center of Rome, this traditional eatery is known for its menu of classic and creative home-cooked pastas and grilled dishes. It's the kind of locals' place where you trust them so much you always order the daily special. Ask them what they recommend, and then take it. Favorites include: Carbonara, Scaloppini with ham and sage, and Noodles with bacon, zucchini and cheese (to die for). Impressive list of Italian wines.

LA TERRAZZA
Via Ludovisi, 49, Rome, +39 06 4781 2752
www.dorchestercollection.com/en/rome/hotel-eden/restaurants-bars/la-terrazza/
CUISINE: Italian
DRINKS: Full Bar
SERVING: Lunch, Dinner; open daily
PRICE RANGE: $$$$
NEIGHBORHOOD: Centro Storico
This eatery, a tourist favorite, offers a beautiful panoramic view of Rome. Menu includes lobster, lamb, steak, and antipasto. Great wine selection. Jackets required.

LE MANI IN PASTA
Via dei Genovesi 37, Rome, +39 06 5816017
www.ristorantedipescetrastevere.roma.it
CUISINE: Italian
DRINKS: Beer & Wine Only
SERVING: Lunch, Dinner; closed Mon
PRICE RANGE: $$$$

NEIGHBORHOOD: Trastevere
This popular rustic eatery offers a menu of classic Italian fare including fresh pastas. Menu favorites include: Tuna tartare, Brasaole with buffalo mozzarella and small gnocchi with clams. Delicious selection of desserts. Reservations recommended because the place is so small. Getting turned away twice because I decided to stop by at the last minute cured me. Now I always book a table. Oh, and ask for a table upstairs or you'll be sent to the basement people can smoke.

LITRO
Via Fratelli Bonnet, 5, +39 06 4544 7639
CUISINE: Italian
DRINKS: Full bar
SERVING: Dinner; Closed Sunday
PRICE RANGE: $$
NEIGHBORHOOD: Monteverde Vecchio
Nice laid back wine bar offering amazing food and wine. It's a small place with only about 20 seats inside, but there's outdoor seating as well. Some people come just for their "natural" wine, but I'm not one of them. It's the food here that stands out. The artichokes are splendid. Usually, in most Roman restaurants, they're either deep-fried or cooked with olive oil. Here, though, the chef serves them the way they do in villages around Italy: thinly sliced raw and sprinkled simply with olive oil & lemon. Nothing beats it. I had 2 orders of this last time I visited.

MACCHERCONI
Piazza delle Coppelle, 44, Rome, +39 06 6830 7895
www.ristorantemaccheroni.com
CUISINE: Roman
DRINKS: Full Bar
SERVING: Lunch, Dinner; open daily
PRICE RANGE: $$
NEIGHBORHOOD: Centro Storico
Not far from the Pantheon you'll find this relaxed eatery offering a menu of homemade Roman cuisine. The place is decorated like an old Roman apartment, with nothing really matching. You'll feel like you're in someone's home. Menu highlights include: Steak, Tripa (a classic Roman dish), and Gnocchi with gorgonzola and pear. Try the tonnarelli, a large type of spaghetti.

MARZAPANE
Via Velletri, 39, +39 06 6478 1692
www.marzapaneroma.com/
CUISINE: Italian
DRINKS: Full bar
SERVING: Lunch/Dinner; Closed Wednesday
PRICE RANGE: $$$$
NEIGHBORHOOD: Pinciano
Chef Alba Ruiz offers customers three different menus (6, 8 and 9 courses). Excellent food with a long list of glowing reviews to prove it. Do try the Spanish-born chef's risotto—it's very different from what you get elsewhere. While most cooks use olive oil for everything, here they use butter, French butter, and the Cantabrian anchovies in the risotto are beyond flavorful.

MUSEO-ATELIER CANOVA TADOLINI
150A-B Via del Babuino, Rome, +39 06 3211 0702
www.canovatadolini.com
CUISINE: Italian
DRINKS: Full Bar
SERVING: Lunch, Late Night, Dinner, Breakfast, Reservations
PRICE RANGE: $$$$
Elegant museum café with a menu of pizzas, finger foods, and pastas. Menu picks include: Tuna steak and Chicken with pistachio. Great place for cocktails before or after a museum visit.

NO.AU
Piazza di Montevecchio, 17, Rome, +39 06 4565 2770

www.noauroma.wordpress.com
CUISINE: Italian
DRINKS: Full Bar
SERVING: Dinner, Late night
PRICE RANGE: $$$
NEIGHBORHOOD:
This tiny bistro serves over 100 varieties of beer. The small menu features bar snacks, steak tartare, and cheese plates. Reservations recommended.

NONNA BETTA
Via del Portico d'Ottavia 16, Rome, +39 06 68806263
www.nonnabetta.it
CUISINE: Jewish, Roman, Middle Eastern
DRINKS: Full Bar
SERVING: Lunch & Dinner; closed Tuesday
PRICE RANGE: $$
NEIGHBORHOOD: Centro Storico
Elegant Italian/Kosher restaurant decorated "old world-style". Favorites: Lasagna with artichokes and Carbonara alla giudia (carbonara Jewish style). Great selection of authentic Jewish cuisine. Don't leave without trying the Jewish style fried artichoke, with its crispy petals and soft pulpy meat.

OPEN BALADIN
Via degli Specchi 6, +39 06 6838989
www.openbaladinroma.it
CUISINE: Burgers
DRINKS: Beer & Wine Only
SERVING: Lunch, Dinner
PRICE RANGE: $$
NEIGHBORHOOD: Centro Storico

This place is actually a pub serving over 100 bottled beers and 40 draught Italian beers. The ever-changing menu includes a wide variety of treats including made-to-order potato chips. The bar grub served here has an American slant: buffalo style chicken wings.

OSTERIA LA GENSOLE
Piazza della Gensola, 15, +39 06 581 6312
www.osterialagensola.it
CUISINE: Roman/Seafood
DRINKS: Beer & Wine Only
SERVING: Lunch, Dinner
PRICE RANGE: $$$
NEIGHBORHOOD: Trastevere
This popular (and still family-run) eatery offers Sicilian fare that makes dining an adventure. The seafood themed menu offers a wide variety of items like the sea bass "ceviche," Carbonara, and fresh tuna "meatballs." Also popular is the spaghetti with sea urchin. Try the tasting menu for a treat.

PASTICCERIA BOCCIONE
Via del Portico D'Ottavia, +39 06 687 8637
No Website
CUISINE: Kosher Bakery/Desserts
DRINKS: No Booze
SERVING: Breakfast & Lunch; closed Sat & Sun
PRICE RANGE: $$
NEIGHBORHOOD: Centro Storico
This Kosher bakery offers an impressive selection desserts including Ricotta cake, plum marmalade and almond crème cake, and dried-fruit cake. You'll also find an assortment of cookies, macaroons, biscotti,

pies, and sweet pizza. Note: most of the fresh pastries sell out by late morning.

PASTIFICIO SAN LORENZO
Via Tiburtina 196, 00199 Rome, +39 06 97273519
www.pastificiocerere.com
CUISINE: Italian
DRINKS: Beer & Wine Only
SERVING: Lunch & Dinner, Dinner only on Saturdays: closed Sundays
PRICE RANGE: $$$
NEIGHBORHOOD: San Lorenzo
Located in a former pasta factory close to the main train station is this upscale dining with an open kitchen. It is part of the Fondazione Cerere, which gives working space to artists—this restaurant and bar is part of their headquarters. Impressive selection of wines – mostly from local wineries. Atmosphere is very nice and there's a hipness to the feel in this place.

PERILLI
Via Marmorata, 39, Rome, +39 06 575 5100
www.trattoria-romana.it/da/perilli
WEBSITE DOWN AT PRESS TIME
CUISINE: Roman/Italian
DRINKS: Full Bar
SERVING: Lunch, Dinner; closed Wed
PRICE RANGE: $$$
NEIGHBORHOOD: Testaccio, Ostiense
Open since 1911, this old style Italian eatery offers special dishes like stewed Roman artichokes and Rigatoni Carbonara (the restaurant's most popular dish). This eatery serves delicious interpretations of classic Italian dishes. Nice wine selection. Bring somebody who speaks Italian or plan on pointing to something on the menu.

PESCHERIA OSTERIA SOR DUILIO
Via delle Cave di Pietralata 44, Rome, +39 06 41787439
www.pescheriasorduilio.com
CUISINE: Seafood
DRINKS: Beer & Wine Only
SERVING: Breakfast, Lunch, & Dinner; closed Mon, Thurs & Sat
PRICE RANGE: $$
NEIGHBORHOOD: Montesacro/Talenti
Not really a restaurant but a fish market that serves raw fish. There's a counter with fish to buy like raw oysters, sushi, and sashimi. Make a reservation if you want a table.

PIATTO ROMANO
Via Giovanni Battista Bodoni 62, Rome, +39 06 64014447

www.piattoromano.com
CUISINE: Roman
DRINKS: Beer & Wine Only
SERVING: Dinner
PRICE RANGE: $$$
NEIGHBORHOOD: Ostiense, Testaccio
Simply decorated eatery offering a limited menu of traditional Roman dishes. Menu picks: Polpette (small meatballs), Lamb sweetbreads, sweet & salty baked cod fish and delicious sautéed anchovies. All the pastas are top-notch. Delicious freshly baked focaccia bread. Not a tourist spot, but English is spoken here.

PIERLUIGI
Piazza de' Ricci 144, Rome, +39 06 6868717
www.pierluigi.it
CUISINE: Italian
DRINKS: Beer & Wine Only
SERVING: Lunch & Dinner, Lunch only on Saturdays; closed Mondays
PRICE RANGE: $$$$

NEIGHBORHOOD: Centro Storico
Authentic Italian eatery offering traditional dishes with an emphasis on seafood specialties prepared perfectly. Favorites: Pasta Carbonara and Prawns carpaccio. Great dining on the terrace overlooking the piazza, where, thankfully, cars re not allowed. Impressive 600 label wine cellar. Heavenly desserts.

PIPERNO
Via Monte de' Cenci 9. Rome, +39 06 68806629
www.ristorantepiperno.it
CUISINE: Roman/Kosher
DRINKS: Beer & Wine Only
SERVING: Lunch & Dinner, Lunch only on Saturdays; closed Mondays
PRICE RANGE: $$$
NEIGHBORHOOD: Centro Storico
This places dates back to 1860, before Italy was even a country, and is a high-end Jewish restaurant (but try to sit outside because it's so nice) serving classic dishes in an old-world setting. Favorites: Gnocchi alla fontina and Bresaola Della Casa. Try the Jewish-style artichoke – you won't be disappointed. Impressive wine list.

PIZZERIA REMO
44 Piazza di Santa Maria Liberatrice, Rome, +39 06 5746270
No Website
CUISINE: Pizza
DRINKS: Beer & Wine Only
SERVING: Dinner, closed Sundays
PRICE RANGE: $$

Popular pizzeria that serves some of the best wood-fired pizza in Rome. Great margarita pizza, eggplant parmesan and fried arancini. Outdoor tables. Cash only. Short wait. Very little English spoken here. but it's always at the top of the "10 best" lists. You'll see why.

PIZZARIUM
Via della Meloria 43, Rome, +39 06 39745416
www.bonci.it
CUISINE: Pizza
DRINKS: Beer & Wine Only
SERVING: Lunch, Dinner
PRICE RANGE: $$
NEIGHBORHOOD: Balduina/Montemario, Prati
This pizzeria offers a great variety (including pizza with almonds and melon) and the pizza is sold per pound. They use a 100-year-old sourdough starter. Different flours are used as well, like kamut and enkir. This is a take-out place so be prepared to stand if you want to eat here.

QUINZI E GABRIELI
Via Delle Coppelle, Rome, +39 06 6879389
www.quinziegabrieli.it
CUISINE: Seafood
DRINKS: Full Bar
SERVING: Lunch, Dinner; closed Sun & Mon
PRICE RANGE: $$$$
NEIGHBORHOOD: Centro Storico
This elegant high-end eatery attracts power players wearing suits because it's close to the parliament and government buildings. The waiter begins pouring

champagne before you even sit at the table. It offers an impressive and elaborate seafood-based menu. There are three beautifully decorated rooms. Guests can order a la carte or select from a prix fixe menu. Try the cuttlefish with crunchy artichokes or one of the many excellent lobster dishes available.

RISTORANTE NINO
11 Via Borgognona, Rome, +39 06 678 6752
www.ristorantenino.it
CUISINE: Italian/Tuscan
DRINKS: Full Bar
SERVING: Lunch & Dinner; closed Wednesdays
PRICE RANGE: $$$$
Upscale Italian eatery specializing in Tuscan dishes. Try the ribollita (a belly-filling bread-and-vegetable soup), the crostini with liver paté. Great classics like Eggplant parmigiana and homemade ravioli. If you want dessert, get the chestnut cake. Nice selection of wines from the owner's estate.

RISTORANTE PIPERNO
Via Monte Dè Cenci, 9, Rome, +39 06 6880 6629
www.ristorantepiperno.it
CUISINE: Roman
DRINKS: Beer & Wine Only
SERVING: Lunch, Dinner
PRICE RANGE: $$$
NEIGHBORHOOD: Centro Storico
This high-end Jewish eatery offers a menu of classic Roman dishes in an old world setting. Menu highlights include: Jewish-style artichokes (an Italian

classic) and Spaghetti with clams. Popular choice for Sunday lunch.

ROMEO
Piazza dell'Emporio, 28, Rome, +39 06 32110120
www.romeo.roma.it
CUISINE: Italian/Roman
DRINKS: Beer & Wine Only
SERVING: Lunch, Dinner
PRICE RANGE: $$$
NEIGHBORHOOD: Prati
This neighborhood pizzeria offers counter service but you can order then eat at the tables. Besides pizza they offers a nice selection of pastas with wonderful sauces and several appetizing meat dishes. Desserts are very good, especially the unique Tiramisu served in a ball-shaped chocolate cover. Nice wine selection.

ROSCIOLI
Via dei Giubbonari, 21, +39 06 6875287

http://www.salumeriaroscioli.com/
CUISINE: Italian
DRINKS: Beer & Wine Only
SERVING: Dinner; closed Sunday
PRICE RANGE: $$
NEIGHBORHOOD: Centro Storico
Formerly a family grocer, now a multipurpose gourmet bodega complete with a wine cellar offering over 2,800 Italian and international wines. Menu features classic Italian dishes with a twist like "brick dough dumplings" and Burrata with caviar. The delicious carbonara is considered by many people to be the best in Rome. Plan to reserve 4 weeks out.

ROSATI
Piazza del Popolo 4/5a, Rome, +39 06 322 5859
www.rosatibar.it
CUISINE: Italian
DRINKS: Full Bar

SERVING: Breakfast, Lunch & Dinner
PRICE RANGE: $$$
NEIGHBORHOOD: Flaminio
High-end art deco Italian restaurant & chocolatiers dating back to the 1920s. Definitely a dining experience as the waiters all wear white tuxedos with white gloves. Favorites: Spaghetti with clams and Tagliatelle with mushrooms. While the best seats are at the outdoor tables overlooking the square, you'll find the Negronis cost 3 times as much in those seats as they do at the inside bar. Nice wine selection.

ROSTI AL PIGNETO
Via Bartolomeo d'Alviano, 65, Rome, +39 06 275 2608
www.rostialpigneto.it
CUISINE: Italian/Burgers
DRINKS: Full Bar
SERVING: Lunch weekends, Dinner nightly
PRICE RANGE: $$
NEIGHBORHOOD: Pigneto
This unique and hip "cooking lab" and Chef Marco Gallotta welcome trendy guests to taste the results of the agricultural research and kitchen. Menu includes veggies, ultra-thin-crust pizzas, 6 variations on the burger, pastas and delicious homemade desserts.

SAID
Via Tiburtina 135, Rome, 39 06 445 9204
www.said.it
CUISINE: Chocolatiers/Desserts
DRINKS: Full Bar
SERVING: Breakfast, Lunch, & Dinner

PRICE RANGE: $$
NEIGHBORHOOD: San Lorenzo
Located in an old chocolate factory, this unique restaurant offers a delicious chocolate-themed menu. Menu highlights include: Tartare with dark chocolate and Tonnarelli with shavings of truffle. Of course there's a large selection of chocolate desserts and sweets to select from.

SBANCO
Via Siria, 1, +39 06 789318
https://sbanco.eatbu.com
CUISINE: Pizza/Italian
DRINKS: Beer & Wine Only
SERVING: Dinner; Closed Monday
PRICE RANGE: $$
NEIGHBORHOOD: Appio San Giovanni
Popular eatery serving great pizzas and Italian fare. I've never been as mad about pizzas (even very good ones) as most Americans, but some friends *dragged* me here, insisting
I had to taste the pizza. (It's rated as one of the top pizza places in all of Rome.) The chef's secret is his domed wood-burning Valoriana oven that keeps the temperature hotter than other ovens. Before baking the dough, he sprinkles little pieces of ice over it. When the oven melts the ice, the surface of the pizza is left wet and a little sticky. OK, it was good. But personally, I like thin-crust pizza. Nice variety of craft beers and local wines.

SALUMERIA-VINERIA ROSIOLI
Via dei Giubbonari 21, Rome +39 06 6875287
www.salumeriaroscioli.com
CUISINE: Italian
DRINKS: Full Bar
SERVING: Lunch, Dinner
PRICE RANGE: $$$
NEIGHBORHOOD: Centro Storico
A very popular wine bar featuring what is really a very traditional menu served in one of the sleekest interior designs in Rome. Menu favorites include: Pork tenderloin and Rigatoni and tomato sauce. Great wine selection.

SETTEMBRINI CAFÉ
Via Luigi Settembrini, 27, Rome, +(39)3232617
www.viasettembrini.it
WEBSITE DOWN AT PRESS TIME
CUISINE: Italian
DRINKS: Full Bar

SERVING: Breakfast, Lunch, & Dinner
PRICE RANGE: $$$$
NEIGHBORHOOD: Prati
The chef's tasting course is a great choice in this upscale modern eatery (with oak plank floors and intimate tables) as it includes treats like raw sea bass with chopped fruit, a sea urchin gelato, rigatoni with anchovies, and seared duck with carrot puree. They offer a buffet lunch, afternoon tea, and full dinner service. Locals who know their wines come here because the extensive selections by the glass are excellent. Perfect place to sit outside in the summer.

SETTIMIO ALL'ARANCIO
Via dell'Arancio, 50, Rome, +39 06 687 6119
www.settimioallarancio.it
CUISINE: Italian
DRINKS: Full Bar
SERVING: Lunch, Dinner; closed Sun
PRICE RANGE: $$$
NEIGHBORHOOD: Centro Storico
This Italian eatery serves their meals family style. It draws people in the media as well as the art world. Italian eateries are not known for their steaks but this one serves delicious steaks like the T-Bone Steak Roman Style. If it's fish you want, get the moist whole fish baked in salt. Dessert selections include a tasty homemade tiramisu.

SETTIMIO AL PELLEGRINO
117 Via del Pellegrino, Rome, +39 06 68801978
www.settimioalpellegrinoroma.it
CUISINE: Italian

DRINKS: Beer & Wine Only
SERVING: Lunch & Dinner; closed Wednesdays
PRICE RANGE: $$
NEIGHBORHOOD: Centro Storico
Charming mom & pop eatery offering a limited menu of Italian classics in two small rooms – one looks into the kitchen. Pop runs the front. Mom runs the kitchen. When I say "limited menu," I mean it. You have to choose from whatever Mom wants to cook that day—usually, you'll get a choice of a couple of pastas and a meat dish and a fish selection. If they have it the day you visit, get the stracciatella (an egg soup that's really special). Favorites: Fettucine with meat sauce and Gnocchi with tomato sauce. Save room for their special dessert - a slice of super sweet Mont Blanc (chestnut and mascarpone meringue). Reservations recommended.

SFORNO
Via Statilio Ottato, 110-116, Rome, +39 06 7154 6118
www.sforno.it
CUISINE: Pizza
DRINKS: Beer & Wine Only
SERVING: Dinner, closed Sun
PRICE RANGE: $$
NEIGHBORHOOD: Tuscolano
This popular eatery offers a great selection of pizzas, fried foods and desserts all homemade. Try the cacao e pepe pizza that's topped with lots of black pepper and a thick layer of pecorino cheese. Great assortment of craft beers.

e pepe pizza that's topped with a thick layer of pecorino cheese. Great assortment of craft beers.

TRATTORIA AL MORO
Vicolo delle Bollette, 13, Rome, +39 06 678 3495
www.ristorantealmororoma.com
CUISINE: Italian
DRINKS: Full Bar
SERVING: Lunch, Dinner; closed Wed & Sun
PRICE RANGE: $$$
NEIGHBORHOOD: Centro Storico
Near the Pantheon and around the corner from the Trevi Fountain is this high-end, wood-paneled restaurant dating back to the late 1920s that has a classic Roman menu with an impressive wine list that attracts a Who's Who of VIPs in Rome. It's better to come here with someone from Rome if you can arrange that. The extensive menu is in Italian but the waiter will assist. Here you'll find a great selection of homemade pastas and sauces like the special Al Moro

pasta with spicy lamb. Look for anything made with *ovoli,* a hard-to-find mushroom. It's delicious.

TRATTORIA DA LUCIA
Vicolo del Mattonato, 2, +39 06 580 3601
CUISINE: Roman
DRINKS: Beer & Wine Only
SERVING: Lunch, Dinner
PRICE RANGE: $$
NEIGHBORHOOD: Trastevere
This place is popular with both locals and tourists (the food is so good the locals put up with the tourists. You have to walk a bit to get here. This trattoria offers up a menu of Roman specialties. My favorite is the Omelet with Parmesan cheese—that's all there is to it, but somehow it's miraculous. Other highlights include Trippa all romana (Tripe with tomato sauce) and Pollo con peperoni (chicken with peppers). , Save room for dessert for they serve what is possibly Rome's best tiramisu. **Cash only**.

TRATTORIA VECCHIA ROMA
Via Ferruccio 12B, Rome, +39 06 4467143
www.trattoriavecchiaroma.it
CUISINE: Italian
DRINKS: Beer & Wine Only
SERVING: Lunch, Dinner; closed Sun
PRICE RANGE: $$
NEIGHBORHOOD: Esquilino
This intimate trattoria offers a menu of classic Italian fare including a variety of bruschettas and pastas. Menu favorites include the tasty Spaghetti Parmigiana.

URBANA 47
Via Urbana, 47, Rome, +39 06 4788 4006
www.urbana47.it
CUISINE: Italian
DRINKS: Full Bar
SERVING: Lunch, Dinner
PRICE RANGE: $$$
NEIGHBORHOOD: Monti
This unique food project unites people in the name of food that celebrates the heritage of the Lazio region. A good way to try the food here is to check out the cocktail hour buffet. Menu includes tapas, pastas, salads, organic lamb, and vegetarian dishes, pumpkin ravioli, fresh pecorino. A favorite of foodies with its impressive ever-changing menu. (They even list the names of their suppliers on the menu.) It's definitely a culinary experience.

NIGHTLIFE

DID YOU FIND AN INTERESTING PLACE?
If you discover a place you think I should check out on my next visit, drop me a line, will you? I'll mention your name if I end up listing it.
andrewdelaplaine@mac.com

IL GOCCETTO
14 Via de Banchi Vecchi, Rome, +39 06 686 4268
www.ilgoccetto.com/en

Popular wine bar – a locals' hangout. Excellent choice of regional wines, salumi and cheeses. They also sell craft Italian beer and Prosecco. Here you can buy a bottle to go.

JERRY THOMAS SPEAKEASY
Vicolo Cellini 30, Rome, +39 370 1146287
www.thejerrythomasproject.it
NEIGHBORHOOD: Centro Storico
Very cool bar and known as one of the best in Rome. Only open Wed-Sat, and they stay open late, till 4. Make a reservation if you want a table (they will give you a special password to use). Bartenders are pro and the cocktails are top notch, so try a couple of different mixed drinks you haven't had in a long time. Here, they will be made perfectly. If this is your first time you'll be charged a 5-euro membership fee.

SHOPPING

DID YOU FIND AN INTERESTING PLACE?
If you discover a place you think I should check out on my next visit, drop me a line, will you? I'll mention your name if I end up listing it.
andrewdelaplaine@mac.com

GELATERIA DEI GRACCHI
272 Via dei Gracchi, Rome, +39 06 321 6668
www.gelateriadeigracchi.it

Popular gelato shop. Flavors change daily and they sell out fast. What makes this place stand apart from other similar shops is its emphasis on different ingredients. **Note: pay** first and take your receipt to the counter to order.

GIOLITTI
40 Via Uffici del Vicario, Rome, +39 06 6991243
www.giolitti.it
This gelato shop (in business for over a century) offers a large variety of flavors. Near the Parthenon. Also available is a nice selection of baked goods, candies, and coffees.

FATAMORGANA
9 Via Lago di Lesina, Rome, +39 06 8639 1589
www.gelateriafatamorgana.com/web/
Here the gelato is smooth, creamy, and light. Nice selection of unique flavors like ginger hazelnut and one called "thought" that is actually grapefruit. Or try the celery-lime or the pimento-chocolate. They sound terrible, but they taste great.

IL GELATO DI CLAUDIO TORCÉ
Viale Aventino, 59, Rome, +39 06 574 6876
WEBSITE DOWN AT PRESS TIME
www.ilgelatodiclaudiotorce.com
Near the Spanish Steps is this great quality gelato shop with a great selection of flavors. They offer 20 varieties of just chocolate. (They have about 100 other flavors.)

PASTICCERIA CINQUE LUNE
89 Corso del Rinascimento, Rome, +39 06 6880 1005
www.cinquelune.net
Bakery offering a nice selection of pastries, cakes, biscuits, chocolates, and cookies. There's a pastry with figs with bay leaf on top that I adore. It's a tiny space with no name on the door, so be careful, you might miss it.

PASTICCERIA LINARI
9 Via Nicola Zabaglia, Rome, +39 06 5782358
www.pasticcerialinari.com
A locals' joint, so if you don't follow the rules you may wait a long time. Pay first and take your receipt to the counter. Great pastries, coffees, lattes, and espresso.

INDEX

A

Al Moro, 9
ALFREDO ALLA SCROFA, 13
ANTICO FORNO AI SERPENTI, 14
ARMANDO AL PANTHEON, 15
AROMA, 16
AROMATICUS, 17

B

BAFFETTO, 17
Bakery, 14, 23

BAR DEL FICO, 18
BIR & FUD, 19
Brasseries, 22
Breakfast, 31, 39
Burgers, 47, 58

C

CACIO E PEPE, 20
Café, 18
CAFÉ DONEY, 20
CASINE VALADIER, 21
CHECCHINO DAL 1887, 21
Chinese, 32
Chocolatiers, 58
COROMANDEL, 22

CRISTALI DI ZUCCHERO, 23

D

DA CESARE, 23
DA ENZO AL 29, 24
DAL BOLOGNESE, 24
Desserts, 48, 58
DITIRANBO, 25

E

EATALY, 26
ENOTECA FERRARA, 27

F

FATAMORGANA, 69
FELICE, 28
FIASCHETTERIA BELTRAMME, 29
FLAVIO AI VELAVEVEDOTTO, 29

G

GELATERIA DEI GRACCHI, 68
GINA, 30
GINGER, 31
GIOLITTI, 69
GLASS HOSTARIA, 31
GREEN T, 32

I

IL CONVIVIO TROIANI, 33
IL GELATO DI CLAUDIO TORCE, 70
IL GOCCETTO, 66
IL MARGUTTA, 34
IL PAGLIACCIO, 34
IL SORPASSO, 35
IL TEMPIO DI ISIDE, 36
IL VERO ALFREDO, 36
Italian, 18, 21, 25, 26, 27, 29, 30, 31, 33, 35, 38, 39, 41, 42, 43, 44, 46, 47, 50, 55, 56, 57, 59, 60, 61, 64, 65
IVO, 37

J

JERRY THOMAS SPEAKEASY, 67

K

Kosher Bakery, 48

L

L'ARCANGELO, 38
LA BUVETTE, 39
LA CAMPANA, 39
LA FOCACCIA, 41
LA MONTECARLO, 40
LA PERGOIA, 41
LA TAVERNE DEI FORI IMPERIALI, 42
LA TERRAZZA, 43
LE MANI IN PASTA, 43
LITRO, 44

M

MACCHERCONI, 45
MARZAPANE, 46
Mediterranean, 36

Modern Cuisine, 16
MUSEO-ATELIER CANOVA TADOLINI, 46

N

NO. AU, 46
NONNA BETTA, 47

O

OPEN BALADIN, 47
OSTERIA LA GENSOLE, 48

P

PALAZZO MANFREDI HOTEL, 16
PASTICCERIA BOCCIONE, 48
PASTICCERIA CINQUE LUNE, 70
PASTICCERIA LINARI, 71
PERILLI, 50
PESCHERIA OSTERIO SOR DUILIO, 51
PIATTO ROMANO, 51
PIERLUIGI, 52
PIPERNO, 53
Pizza, 17, 19, 40, 42, 53, 54, 59, 62
PIZZARIUM, 54
PIZZERIA REMO, 53

Q

QUINZI E GABRIELI, 54

R

RISTORANTE NINO, 55
RISTORANTE PIPERNO, 55
Roman, 28, 30, 45, 48, 50, 56, 64
ROMEO, 56
ROSATI, 57
ROSCIOLI, 56
ROSTI AL PIGNETO, 58

S

SAID, 58
SALUMERIA-VINERIA ROSIOLI, 60
SBANCO, 59
Seafood, 48, 51, 54
SETTEMBRINI CAFÉ, 60
SETTIMIO AL PELLEGRINO, 61
SETTIMIO ALL'ARANCIO, 61
SFORNO, 62

T

TRATTORIA AL MORO, 63
TRATTORIA DA LUCIA, 64
TRATTORIA VECCHIA ROMA, 64
Tre Scalini, 10
Tuscan, 55

U

URBANA 47, 65

V

Vegetarian, 34

WANT 3 FREE THRILLERS?

Why, of course you do!
If you like these writers--
Vince Flynn, Brad Thor, Tom Clancy, James Patterson, David Baldacci, John Grisham, Brad Meltzer, Daniel Silva, Don DeLillo
If you like these TV series –
House of Cards, Scandal, West Wing, The Good Wife, Madam Secretary, Designated Survivor

You'll love the **unputdownable** series about Jack Houston St. Clair, with political intrigue, romance, and loads of action and suspense.

Besides writing travel books, I've written political thrillers for many years that have delighted hundreds of thousands of readers. I want to introduce you to my work!
Send me an email and I'll send you a link where you can download the first 3 books in my bestselling series, absolutely FREE.
Mention **this book** when you email me.
andrewdelaplaine@mac.com

www.ingramcontent.com/pod-product-compliance
Lightning Source LLC
LaVergne TN
LVHW051511070426
835507LV00022B/3048